Easy Ways to Make Money Online

Unlock Your Earning Potential: Simple Strategies for Online Success

Kitchen Mage

The target audiences

1. Aspiring Entrepreneurs: Individuals looking to start their online businesses but seeking straightforward methods to generate income.
2. Stay-at-Home Parents: Parents interested in earning extra income while managing household responsibilities.
3. Freelancers: Freelancers seeking additional revenue streams or more stable income opportunities online.
4. College Students: Students searching for flexible ways to earn money while studying or during breaks.
5. Retirees: Retired individuals interested in supplementing their retirement income through simple online ventures.
6. Side Hustlers: People with full-time jobs looking for easy online side hustles to increase their income.
7. Digital Nomads: Individuals who prioritize location independence and are

seeking simple ways to sustain their lifestyle online.

8. Novice Internet Users: People new to the online space who want straightforward guidance on making money online.

9. Creative Professionals: Artists, writers, designers, and musicians looking for accessible avenues to monetize their talents online.

10. Social Media Influencers: Individuals with a significant online following interested in exploring additional income streams beyond traditional sponsorships.

11. Solopreneurs: Independent professionals such as coaches, consultants, and trainers seeking easy-to-implement online monetization strategies.

12. Remote Workers: Employees working remotely who want to explore supplementary income opportunities during their free time.

13. Budget-Conscious Individuals: People on tight budgets looking for low-cost or free methods to earn money online.

14. Career Changers: Individuals transitioning to new industries or careers seeking flexible online income options as they navigate their transition.
15. Digital Marketing Enthusiasts: Individuals passionate about digital marketing interested in leveraging their skills to create online revenue streams.

Table of Contents

I. Introduction

- Welcome readers to the world of online income generation
- A brief overview of the book's purpose: to provide actionable strategies for making money online easily

II. Understanding the Online Landscape

- Exploring the vast opportunities available for making money online
- Discussing the benefits of online income, such as flexibility, scalability, and global reach

III. Setting the Foundation

- Defining personal goals and objectives for online income generation

- Addressing common misconceptions and fears about making money online
- Cultivating the right mindset for success in the digital world

IV. Exploring Profitable Online Ventures

1. Freelancing Fundamentals
   - Introduction to freelancing and its various niches
   - Tips for identifying marketable skills and services
   - Strategies for finding clients and building a sustainable freelancing career
2. E-commerce Essentials
   - Overview of e-commerce business models (dropshipping, print-on-demand, etc.)
   - Step-by-step guide to setting up an online store

- Techniques for driving traffic and increasing sales

3. Affiliate Marketing Mastery
   - Understanding the basics of affiliate marketing
   - Finding profitable affiliate programs and products to promote
   - Implementing effective promotion strategies to maximize earnings

4. Content Monetization Methods
   - Exploring different content creation platforms (blogging, YouTube, podcasting)
   - Strategies for monetizing content through advertising, sponsorships, and digital products
   - Tips for building a loyal audience and increasing revenue streams

5. Passive Income Pathways
   - Introduction to passive income opportunities (investing, rental income, royalties)

- Tips for building passive income streams that generate revenue while you sleep
  - Understanding the importance of diversification and long-term wealth-building

V. Overcoming Challenges and Staying Motivated

- Common obstacles faced by aspiring online earners
- Techniques for overcoming self-doubt, procrastination, and burnout
- Inspiring stories of individuals who overcame challenges to achieve online success

VI. Taking Action: Your Roadmap to Success

- Creating a personalized action plan based on individual goals and interests

- Setting SMART goals and breaking them down into actionable steps
- Resources and tools to support readers on their journey to online success

VII. Conclusion

- Recap of key insights and strategies covered in the book
- Encouragement to take the first step towards unlocking earning potential online
- Final words of motivation and empowerment for readers embarking on their online income journey

Introduction

Welcome to the exciting world of online income generation. In today's digital age, the internet offers unprecedented opportunities for individuals to earn money from the comfort of their own homes. Whether you're looking to supplement your existing income, achieve financial independence, or pursue your entrepreneurial dreams, the online realm presents a wealth of possibilities waiting to be explored.

In this book, we aim to serve as your guide on this journey towards financial empowerment. Our primary goal is to equip you with actionable strategies that will enable you to make money online easily and effectively. We understand that the prospect of diving into the vast ocean of online opportunities can be overwhelming, which is why we have distilled our expertise and experience into practical, step-by-step guidance. Throughout the pages of this book, you will find a comprehensive overview of the various avenues for online income generation, ranging from freelancing and e-commerce to affiliate marketing and passive income streams. We will delve into the fundamentals of each method, providing you with the knowledge and tools necessary to embark on your online income journey with confidence.

Moreover, we recognize the importance of simplicity and accessibility in today's fast-paced world. That's why our strategies are designed to be straightforward to implement, regardless of your prior experience or technical expertise. Whether you're a seasoned entrepreneur or a complete novice, you'll find valuable insights and practical advice tailored to your needs.

So, if you're ready to unlock your earning potential and take control of your financial future, then join us as we explore the limitless possibilities of making money online. Together, we'll navigate the digital landscape and pave the way towards your success in the online arena. Let's embark on this journey together and turn your dreams of financial freedom into reality.

II. Understanding the Online Landscape

In today's interconnected world, the internet serves as a bustling marketplace teeming with opportunities for individuals to capitalize on their skills, talents, and passions. From freelancing platforms and e-commerce websites to affiliate marketing programs and content creation platforms, the online landscape offers a diverse array of avenues for making money. One of the most compelling aspects of online income generation is the sheer breadth of opportunities available. Whether you're a writer, designer, programmer, or entrepreneur, there is a niche waiting to be explored and monetized online. From providing services to selling products or creating digital content, the possibilities are virtually endless.

Moreover, online income offers a range of benefits that traditional employment may not provide. One of the key advantages is flexibility. Unlike traditional nine-to-five jobs, online income opportunities allow individuals to set their schedules and work from anywhere with an internet connection. This flexibility is particularly appealing to those seeking a better work-life balance or looking to supplement their existing income without sacrificing their freedom.

In addition to flexibility, online income also offers scalability. With the right strategies and resources, individuals can scale their online businesses and income streams exponentially. Whether it's expanding product lines, reaching new audiences, or diversifying revenue streams, the internet provides a platform for unlimited growth potential.

Another significant benefit of online income is its global reach. Unlike brick-and-mortar businesses limited by geographical constraints, online businesses can reach customers and clients from around the world. This global reach not only expands market opportunities but also fosters cultural exchange and collaboration on a global scale.

In summary, understanding the online landscape involves recognizing the vast array of

opportunities available for making money online
and embracing the benefits that online income
offers, including flexibility, scalability, and
global reach. By leveraging these advantages
and tapping into the wealth of opportunities
available online, individuals can unlock their
earning potential and achieve financial success
in the digital age.

III. Setting the Foundation

Before embarking on your journey into the world of online income generation, it is essential to lay a solid foundation that will support your efforts and propel you towards success. This foundation involves three crucial steps: defining your goals, addressing misconceptions and fears, and cultivating the right mindset.

1. Defining Personal Goals and Objectives
The first step in setting the foundation for your online income journey is to define your personal goals and objectives. What do you hope to achieve through online income generation? Are you looking to supplement your existing income, achieve financial independence, or pursue your entrepreneurial dreams?

By clearly defining your goals, you can tailor your approach to online income generation to align with your aspirations. Whether you're aiming to earn a specific amount of money each month, build a sustainable online business, or simply explore new opportunities, having a clear vision of your objectives will guide your decisions and actions moving forward.

2. Addressing Common Misconceptions and Fears

Making money online can be daunting, especially for those who are unfamiliar with the digital landscape. Common misconceptions and fears, such as the belief that online income is unreliable or that success is reserved for a select few, can hold individuals back from pursuing their online income goals.

It is essential to address these misconceptions and fears head-on and recognize them as barriers to success. The truth is that while making money online may require effort and perseverance, it is entirely achievable for anyone willing to put in the work. By challenging these misconceptions and reframing your mindset, you can approach online income generation with confidence and determination.

3. Cultivating the Right Mindset for Success

Success in the digital world requires more than just technical skills or business acumen; it also requires the right mindset. Cultivating a mindset of resilience, adaptability, and continuous learning is essential for navigating the challenges and opportunities of the online landscape.

This mindset involves embracing failure as a learning opportunity, staying open to new ideas and strategies, and maintaining a positive attitude even in the face of setbacks. By cultivating a growth mindset and adopting an entrepreneurial spirit, you can overcome obstacles, seize opportunities, and ultimately achieve success in the digital world.

In summary, setting the foundation for online income generation involves defining your personal goals, addressing misconceptions and fears, and cultivating the right mindset for success. By laying this groundwork, you can embark on your online income journey with clarity, confidence, and purpose, setting yourself up for success in the dynamic and ever-evolving digital landscape.

IV. Exploring Profitable Online Ventures

In this section, we will delve into various lucrative opportunities for generating income online. From freelancing and e-commerce to affiliate marketing, content creation, and passive income streams, we will explore the fundamentals of each venture and provide actionable strategies for success.

1. Freelancing Fundamentals

Introduction to Freelancing: Freelancing offers individuals the opportunity to leverage their skills and expertise to provide services to clients on a project basis. We will explore the diverse niches within freelancing, including writing, graphic design, programming, and more.

Tips for Identifying Marketable Skills: We will discuss how to identify your strengths and marketable skills that are in demand within the freelancing market. Whether you're a seasoned professional or just starting, there are opportunities to thrive in the freelancing world.

Strategies for Finding Clients: Finding clients is essential for building a sustainable freelancing career. We will provide practical strategies for marketing your services, networking with potential clients, and leveraging freelancing platforms to connect with opportunities.

Building a Sustainable Freelancing Career: Building a sustainable freelancing career requires more than just finding clients. We will discuss the importance of delivering high-quality work, building relationships with clients, and managing your time and workload effectively.

2. E-commerce Essentials

Overview of E-commerce Business Models: E-commerce offers a range of business models, including dropshipping, print-on-demand, and traditional online retail. We will provide an overview of each model, highlighting their advantages and challenges.

Step-by-Step Guide to Setting Up an Online Store: Setting up an online store can seem daunting, but it doesn't have to be. We will walk you through the process, from choosing a platform and designing your store to managing inventory and processing orders.

Techniques for Driving Traffic and Increasing Sales: Once your store is up and running, the next challenge is driving traffic and converting visitors into customers. We will discuss proven techniques for attracting visitors to your store, optimizing your product listings, and maximizing sales.

3. Affiliate Marketing Mastery

Understanding the Basics of Affiliate Marketing: Affiliate marketing involves promoting products or services and earning a commission for each sale or referral made through your unique affiliate link. We will explain the fundamentals of affiliate marketing and how it works.

Finding Profitable Affiliate Programs: Not all affiliate programs are created equal. We will show you how to find high-paying affiliate programs and products that align with your audience and interests.

Implementing Effective Promotion Strategies: Success in affiliate marketing requires more than just sharing affiliate links. We will share proven strategies for promoting affiliate products effectively, including content marketing, email marketing, and social media promotion.

4. Content Monetization Methods

Exploring Different Content Creation Platforms: Content creation offers endless possibilities for monetization, from blogging and YouTube to podcasting and beyond. We will explore the different platforms available and how to choose the right one for your content.

Strategies for Monetizing Content: Once you've created valuable content, the next step is monetization. We will discuss various monetization strategies, including advertising, sponsorships, affiliate marketing, and selling digital products.

Building a Loyal Audience: Building a loyal audience is essential for long-term success in content creation. We will share tips for attracting and engaging your audience, building trust and credibility, and fostering a community around your content.

5. Passive Income Pathways

Introduction to Passive Income Opportunities: Passive income offers the promise of earning money while you sleep. We will introduce various passive income opportunities, including investing, rental income, royalties, and more.

Tips for Building Passive Income Streams: Building passive income streams requires upfront effort and investment, but the rewards can be significant. We will provide practical tips for getting started with passive income, including diversification and long-term wealth-building strategies.

Understanding the Importance of Diversification: Diversification is key to building sustainable passive income streams. We will discuss the importance of diversifying your income sources to mitigate risk and maximize returns over the long term.

By exploring these profitable online ventures and implementing the strategies outlined, you can unlock your earning potential and achieve success in the digital economy. Whether you're looking to build a freelancing career, launch an e-commerce store, become an affiliate marketer, monetize your content, or build passive income streams, the opportunities are endless. It's time to take action and seize the opportunities that await you in the world of online income generation.

V. Overcoming Challenges and Staying Motivated

As you embark on your journey into the world of online income generation, it's important to recognize that challenges and obstacles are inevitable. However, with the right mindset and strategies, you can overcome these challenges and stay motivated to achieve your goals. In this section, we will explore common obstacles faced by aspiring online earners, techniques for overcoming self-doubt, procrastination, and burnout, and inspiring stories of individuals who have overcome challenges to achieve online success.

1. Common Obstacles Faced by Aspiring Online Earners

- Lack of Experience: Many aspiring online earners may feel overwhelmed by their lack of experience in the digital realm. Whether it's technical skills, marketing knowledge, or business acumen, feeling ill-equipped can be a significant barrier to success.

- Fear of Failure: The fear of failure is another common obstacle that can hold individuals back from pursuing their online income goals. The fear of making mistakes or not achieving desired results can paralyze individuals and prevent them from taking action.
- Competition: The online marketplace is crowded with competitors vying for attention and customers. Standing out from the crowd and gaining traction can be challenging, especially in saturated niches.

2. Techniques for Overcoming Self-Doubt, Procrastination, and Burnout

- Cultivate Self-Confidence: Building self-confidence is essential for overcoming self-doubt. Focus on your strengths, celebrate your successes, and remind yourself of past achievements to bolster your confidence.
- Set Clear Goals and Deadlines: Break down your goals into smaller, actionable steps and set deadlines for each task. This

will help you stay focused and motivated, reducing the likelihood of procrastination.

- Practice Self-Care: Prioritize self-care to prevent burnout. Make time for activities that recharge your batteries, such as exercise, hobbies, and spending time with loved ones. Remember that taking breaks and practicing self-compassion are essential for long-term success.

3. Inspiring Stories of Individuals Who Overcame Challenges to Achieve Online Success

- Sarah's Story: Sarah struggled with self-doubt and imposter syndrome when she started her freelance writing career. Despite her fears, she persevered, honed her skills, and gradually built a thriving freelancing business. Today, Sarah is a sought-after writer, earning a comfortable income while doing what she loves.
- David's Journey: David faced numerous setbacks and failures in his e-commerce business before finding success. Instead of giving up, he learned from his mistakes,

pivoted when necessary, and remained resilient in the face of adversity. Today, David's e-commerce store is a profitable venture, providing him with financial stability and freedom.

- Emma's Triumph: Emma struggled with burnout and was overwhelmed while building her passive income streams. However, with perseverance and a commitment to self-care, she was able to overcome these challenges and create multiple streams of passive income. Today, Emma enjoys a flexible lifestyle, earning passive income while pursuing her passions and spending time with her family.

In conclusion, overcoming challenges and staying motivated is an essential aspect of achieving success in the world of online income generation. By recognizing common obstacles, implementing techniques to overcome self-doubt and procrastination, and drawing inspiration from the stories of others, you can navigate the ups and downs of the journey and ultimately achieve your online income goals. Remember that perseverance, resilience, and a positive mindset are key to realizing your dreams in the digital economy.

VI. Taking Action: Your Roadmap to Success

As you embark on your journey towards online success, taking action is paramount. In this section, we will guide you through the process of creating a personalized action plan, setting SMART goals, and providing resources and tools to support you on your path to online success.

1. Creating a Personalized Action Plan
Creating a personalized action plan begins with identifying your individual goals and interests. Take some time to reflect on what you hope to achieve through your online endeavors. Are you looking to build a freelancing career, launch an e-commerce store, or monetize your content? Once you have a clear vision of your goals, tailor your action plan to align with your aspirations, strengths, and preferences. Consider factors such as your skills, resources, and time availability when crafting your action plan. Break down your goals into smaller, manageable tasks, and prioritize them based on

their importance and urgency. By creating a roadmap tailored to your specific needs and circumstances, you can chart a clear path toward online success.

2. Setting SMART Goals and Breaking Them Down into Actionable Steps

Setting SMART goals is essential for turning your aspirations into reality. SMART goals are Specific, Measurable, Achievable, Relevant, and Time-bound. By following this framework, you can ensure that your goals are clear, realistic, and attainable.

Once you have defined your SMART goals, break them down into actionable steps. Identify the specific actions you need to take to achieve each goal and assign deadlines to each task. Breaking your goals down into smaller, actionable steps not only makes them more manageable but also provides a roadmap for progress and accountability.

3. Resources and Tools to Support Your Journey to Online Success

Building an online business or generating income online requires access to the right resources and tools. Fortunately, there are a plethora of resources available to support you on your journey to online success.

- Educational Resources: Take advantage of online courses, tutorials, and educational materials to expand your knowledge and skills in your chosen niche. Platforms like Udemy, Coursera, and Skillshare offer a wide range of courses on topics such as freelancing, e-commerce, digital marketing, and more.
- Networking Opportunities: Connect with like-minded individuals and industry experts through online communities, forums, and social media groups. Networking can provide valuable insights, opportunities for collaboration, and support from peers who understand the challenges and triumphs of the online business world.
- Productivity Tools: Utilize productivity tools and software to streamline your workflow, manage your time effectively, and stay organized. Tools like Trello,

Asana, and Evernote can help you plan and track your progress towards your goals.

- Marketing Platforms: Whether you're promoting your freelancing services, e-commerce store, or content, leverage marketing platforms to reach your target audience. Platforms like Google Ads, Facebook Ads, and Instagram can help you drive traffic, generate leads, and increase sales.

By leveraging these resources and tools, you can enhance your skills, expand your network, and optimize your online efforts for maximum success.

In conclusion, taking action is the key to realizing your dreams of online success. By creating a personalized action plan, setting SMART goals, and utilizing resources and tools to support your journey, you can overcome obstacles, stay focused, and achieve your goals in the dynamic and ever-evolving world of online business. Remember that consistency, perseverance, and a willingness to learn are

essential qualities for success in the digital
economy.

VII. Conclusion

As we come to the end of this journey through the world of online income generation, it's essential to reflect on the key insights and strategies covered in this book. From exploring profitable online ventures to overcoming challenges and staying motivated, we have provided you with the knowledge and tools necessary to embark on your online income journey with confidence and determination. Recap of Key Insights and Strategies Throughout this book, we have explored a variety of profitable online ventures, including freelancing, e-commerce, affiliate marketing, content creation, and passive income streams. We have discussed the fundamentals of each venture, provided practical tips and strategies for success, and shared inspiring stories of individuals who have achieved online success. We have addressed common obstacles and challenges faced by aspiring online earners, such as self-doubt, procrastination, and burnout, and provided techniques for overcoming these obstacles and staying motivated. We have emphasized the importance of setting clear goals, creating a personalized action plan, and leveraging resources and tools to support your journey to online success.

Encouragement to Take the First Step

Now that you have gained valuable insights and strategies for making money online, it's time to take the first step step tracking your earning potential. Whether you're a seasoned entrepreneur or a complete novice, remember that every journey begins with a single step. Don't let fear or uncertainty hold you back from pursuing your online income goals. Trust in your abilities, embrace the opportunities that await you, and take action towards realizing your dreams.

Final Words of Motivation and Empowerment

As you embark on your online income journey, remember that success is not guaranteed overnight. It takes time, effort, and perseverance to build a sustainable online business or generate income online. Stay committed to your goals, stay flexible in your approach, and stay resilient in the face of challenges.

Believe in yourself and your ability to succeed in the digital economy. You have the knowledge, the skills, and the determination to achieve your online income goals. Trust in the process, stay focused on your vision never lose sight of the possibilities that lie ahead.

In closing, I encourage you to embrace the opportunities of the digital age, unleash your potential, and pursue your dreams with passion and purpose. Your journey to online success begins now. Take that first step, and let your entrepreneurial spirit soar. The possibilities are limitless, and the rewards are waiting for you. Go forth with confidence, and may your online income journey be filled with abundance, fulfillment, and success.